# THE GO-GETTER

# THE
# GO-GETTER

*A Story That Tells You How to Be One*

---

# PETER B. KYNE

*with*

ALAN AXELROD

*A Revised Edition of the Classic Story*

TIMES BOOKS

Henry Holt and Company ✳ New York

Times Books
Henry Holt and Company, LLC
*Publishers since 1866*
115 West 18th Street
New York, New York 10011

Henry Holt® is a registered trademark of
Henry Holt and Company, LLC.

Library of Congress Cataloging-in-Publication Data
Kyne, Peter B. (Peter Bernard), 1880–1957.
  The go-getter : a story that tells you how to be one / Peter B.
Kyne with Alan Axelrod.—Rev. ed.
    p.    cm.
"A revised edition of the classic story."
  ISBN 0-8050-6562-8 (hb.)
    1. Motivation (Psychology)—Fiction. 2. Success in business—
Fiction. 3. Businessmen—Fiction. I. Axelrod, Alan, 1952– II. Title.
PS3521.Y5 G6 2003
813'.52—dc21                                    2002031952

Revised Edition 2003

Designed by Kelly S. Too

Printed in the United States of America

3   5   7   9   10   8   6   4   2

*This little book is dedicated to
the memory of my dead chief,
Brigadier-General Leroy S. Lyon,
sometime commander of the
65th Field Artillery Brigade,
40th Division, United States Army.*

*He practiced and preached a religion
of loyalty to the country and the
appointed task, whatever it might be.*

*—Peter B. Kyne*

# THE GO-GETTER

## · I ·

MR. ALDEN P. RICKS, KNOWN IN PACIFIC COAST
wholesale lumber and shipping circles as Cappy
Ricks, had more troubles than a hen with ducklings.
He remarked as much to Mr. Skinner, president and
general manager of the Ricks Logging & Lumbering Company, the corporate entity which represented Cappy's vast lumber interests; and he fairly
barked the information at Captain Matt Peasley, his
son-in-law and also president and manager of the
Blue Star Navigation Company, another corporate
entity which represented the Ricks interest in the
American mercantile marine.

Mr. Skinner received this information in silence.
He was not related to Cappy Ricks. But Matt

Peasley sat down, crossed his legs and matched glares with his mercurial father-in-law.

"*You* have troubles!" he jeered, with emphasis on the pronoun. "Have you got a misery in your back, or is Herbert Hoover the wrong man for Secretary of Commerce?"

"Stow your sarcasm, young feller," Cappy shrilled. "You know dad-blamed well it isn't a question of health or politics. It's the fact that in my old age I find myself totally surrounded by the choicest aggregation of mental duds since Ajax defied the lightning."

"Meaning whom?"

"You and Skinner."

"Why, what have we done?"

"You argued me into taking on the management of twenty-five of those infernal Shipping Board freighters, and no sooner did we have them allocated to us than a near panic hits the country, freight rates go to glory, marine engineers go on strike and every infernal young whelp we send out to take charge of one of our offices in Asia promptly gets the swelled head and thinks he's divinely ordained to drink up all the synthetic Scotch whiskey manufactured in Japan for the benefit of thirsty Americans. In my old age you two have forced us into the position of having to fire folks by cable. Why? Because we're breaking into a game that isn't being played on the home grounds. A lot of our business is so far away we can't control it."

Matt Peasley leveled an accusing finger at Cappy Ricks. "We never argued you into taking over the management of those Shipping Board boats. We argued me into it. I'm the goat. You have nothing to do with it. You retired ten years ago. All the troubles in the marine end of this shop belong on my capable shoulders, old settler."

"Theoretically—yes. Actually—no. I hope you do not expect me to abandon mental as well as physical effort. Great Wampus Cats! Am I to be denied a sentimental interest in matters where I have a controlling financial interest? I admit you two boys are running my affairs and ordinarily you run them rather well, but—but—ahem! Harumph-h-h! What's the matter with you, Matt? And you, also, Skinner? If Matt makes a mistake, it's your job to remind him of it before the results manifest themselves, is it not? And vice versa. Have you two lost your ability to judge men and yourselves, or did you ever have such ability?"

"You're referring to Henderson in the Shanghai office, I dare say," Mr. Skinner cut in.

"I am, Skinner. And I'm here to remind you that if we'd stuck to our own game, which is coastwise shipping, and had left the trans-Pacific field with its general cargoes to others, we wouldn't have any Shanghai office at this moment and we would not be pestered by the Hendersons of this world."

"He's the best lumber salesman we've ever had," Mr. Skinner defended. "And the Pacific market is still untapped. I had every hope that he would send us orders for many a cargo for Asiatic delivery."

"And he had gone through every job in this office, from office boy to sales manager in the lumber department and even passenger agent in the navigation company." Matt Peasley supplemented.

"I admit all of that. But did you consult me when you decided to send him out to China on his own?"

"Of course not. I'm boss of the Blue Star Navigation Company, am I not? The man was in charge of the Shanghai office before you ever opened your mouth to discharge your cargo of free advice."

"I told you then that Henderson wouldn't make good, didn't I?"

"You did."

"And now I have an opportunity to tell you the

little tale you didn't give me an opportunity to tell you before you sent him out. Henderson *was* a good man—a crackerjack man—when he had a better man over him. But—I've been twenty years reducing a tendency on the part of that fellow's head to bust his hat-band. And now he's gone south with a hundred and thirty thousand taels of our Shanghai bank account."

"Permit me to remind you, Mr. Ricks," Mr. Skinner cut in coldly, "that he was bonded to the extent of a quarter of a million dollars."

"Not a peep out of you, Skinner. Not a peep. Permit me to remind *you* that I'm the little genius who placed that insurance."

"Well, I must admit your far-sightedness in that instance will keep the Shanghai office going this year," Matt Peasley replied. "However, we face this situation, Cappy. Henderson has wined and dined in excess of his salary. He's attended to the wrong business at the wrong time and he's capped his inefficiency by spending our bank account on who knows what. We couldn't foresee that. When we send a man out to Asia to be our manager there, we have to trust him all the way or not at all. There is no use weeping over spilled milk, Cappy. Our job is to select a successor to Henderson and send him out to Shanghai on the next boat to clean things up and get things in order."

"Oh, very well, Matt," Cappy replied magnanimously, "I'll not rub it into you. I suppose I'm far from generous, bawling you out like this. Perhaps, when you're my age and have a lot of mental and moral weaklings nip you and draw blood as often as they've drawn it on me you'll be a better judge than I of men worthy of the weight of responsibility. Skinner, have you got a candidate for this job?"

"I regret to say, sir, I have not. All of the men in my department are quite young—too young for the responsibility."

"What do you mean—young?" Cappy blazed.

"Well, the only man I would consider for the job is Andrews and he doesn't have the experience— he's only about thirty, I should say."

"About thirty, eh? Strikes me you were about twenty-eight when I threw ten thousand a year at you in actual cash, and a couple of million dollars' worth of responsibility."

"Yes, sir, but then Andrews has never been tested—"

"Skinner," Cappy interrupted in his most awful voice, "it's a constant source of amazement to me why I refrain from firing you. You say Andrews has never been tested. Why hasn't he been tested? Why are we maintaining untested material in this shop, anyhow? Eh? Answer me that. Tut, tut, tut! Not a peep out of you, sir. If you had done your duty, you would have taken a year's vacation when lumber was selling itself in 1919 and 1920, and you would have left Andrews sitting in at your desk to see the sort of stuff he's made of."

"It's a mighty lucky thing I didn't go away for a year," Skinner protested respectfully, "because the market broke—like that—and if you don't think we have to hustle to sell sufficient lumber these days to keep our own ships busy freighting it—"

"Skinner, how old was Matt Peasley when I turned over the Blue Star Navigation Company to him, lock, stock, and barrel? Why, he wasn't twenty-six years old. Skinner, are you so removed from those days that you don't remember the way I tested you both? When did you become a killjoy, throttling the neck of industry with absurd theories that a man's back must be bent like an ox-bow and his locks snowy-white before he can be entrusted with responsibility and a living wage? This is a smart man's world, a persistent man's world, not an old man's world, Skinner, and don't you ever forget it. And the go-getters of this world are as often as not under thirty years of age. Matt," he concluded, turning to his son-in-law, "what do you think of Andrews for that Shanghai job?"

"I think he'll do."

"Why do you think he'll do?"

"Because he ought to do. He's been with us long enough to have acquired sufficient knowledge and experience to enable him—"

"Has he acquired the courage to tackle the job, Matt?" Cappy interrupted. "That's more important than this doggoned experience you and Skinner prate so much about."

"I know nothing of his courage. I assume that he has force and initiative. I know he has a pleasing personality."

"Well, before we send him out we ought to know whether or no he has force and initiative."

"Then," quoth Matt Peasley, rising, "I need a few more months to find Henderson's successor. Unless you can name the lucky man."

"Yes, indeed," Skinner agreed. "I'm sure it's quite beyond my poor abilities to uncover Andrews' force and initiative on such short notice. He does possess sufficient force and initiative for his present job, but—"

"But will he possess force and initiative when he has to make quick decisions six thousand miles from expert advice, and stand or fall by that decision? That's what we want to know, Skinner."

"I suggest, sir," Mr. Skinner replied with politeness, "that you conduct the examination."

"I accept the nomination, Skinner. By the Holy Pink-toed Prophet! The next man we send out to that Shanghai office is going to be a go-getter. We've had three managers go rotten on us and that's three too many."

And without further ado, Cappy swung his aged legs up on to his desk and slid down in his swivel chair until he rested on his spine. His head sank on his breast and he closed his eyes.

"He's framing the examination for Andrews," Matt Peasley whispered, as he and Skinner made their exits.

# · II ·

THE CHAIRMAN AND PRESIDENT EMERITUS OF the Ricks interests was not destined to uninterrupted cogitation, however. Within ten minutes his private exchange operator called him to the telephone.

"What is it?" Cappy yelled into the transmitter.

"There is a young man in the general office. His name is Mr. William E. Peck and he desires to see you personally."

Cappy sighed. "Oh, so he desires to see me personally? Who is he?" Cappy rolled back into his chair while he waited for the operator to crackle through the response.

"He says he was with our brightest competitor,

and wants to tell you how he got your people in the Middle West scurrying a few years ago."

This got Cappy's attention. "Very well," he replied. "Have him shown in."

Almost immediately the office boy ushered Mr. Peck into Cappy's presence. The moment he was fairly inside the door the visitor halted, came easily and naturally to "attention" and bowed respectfully, while the cool glance of his keen blue eyes held steadily the autocrat of the Blue Star Navigation Company.

"Mr. Ricks, William E. Peck is my name, sir. Thank you for acceding to my request for an interview."

"Ahem! Hum-m-m!" Cappy looked belligerent. "Sit down, Mr. Peck."

Mr. Peck sat down, but as he crossed to the chair beside Cappy's desk, the old gentleman noticed that his visitor walked with a slight limp, and that his left forearm had been amputated half way to the elbow. To the observant Cappy, the American Legion button in Mr. Peck's lapel told the story.

"Well, Mr. Peck," he queried, "what can I do for you?"

"I've called for my job," the veteran replied briefly.

"By the Holy Pink-toed Prophet!" Cappy ejaculated, "you say that like a man who doesn't expect to be refused."

"Quite right, sir. I do not anticipate a refusal."

"Why?"

Mr. William E. Peck's engaging features rippled into the most compelling smile Cappy Ricks had ever seen. "I am a salesman, Mr. Ricks," he replied. "I know that statement to be true because I have demonstrated, over a period of five years, that I can sell my share of anything that has a hockable value. I have always found, however, that before proceeding to sell goods I had to sell the manufacturer of those goods something, to wit—myself! I am about to sell myself to you."

"Mr. Peck," said Cappy smilingly, "you win. You've sold me already. When did they sell you a membership in the military forces of the United States of America?"

"The morning after we joined the fray, sir. April 7, 1917."

"I soldiered with the Knights of Columbus at Camp Kearny myself, but when they refused to let me go abroad with my division my heart was broken, so I went over the hill."

That little touch of the language of the line

warmed Mr. Peck's heart considerably. "Yes, Mr. Ricks, I know the tale," he replied with feeling. "I was with the Portland Lumber Company, selling lumber in the Middle West before the war," he explained. "The surest way to give your competitors a run is to know your competitors better than they know themselves. I made it a habit to know what your salesmen and your managers and you were up to. It became such a habit it was hard to shake even after I signed up."

Cappy nodded his head.

"Uncle Sam gave me my discharge at Letterman General Hospital last week, with half disability on my ten thousand dollars' worth of government insurance. My arm was a loss, but I soon learned to navigate without it. My broken leg though was a long time mending, and now it's shorter than it really ought to be. And I developed pneumonia with influenza and they found some TB indications after that. I've been at the government tuberculosis hospital at Fort Bayard, New Mexico, for a year. However, what's left of me is certified to be sound. I'm ready to get back in the saddle."

"Not at all blue or discouraged?" Cappy hazarded.

"Oh, I got off easy, Mr. Ricks. I have my head

left—and my right arm. I can think and I can write, and even if one of my wheels is flat, I can hike longer and faster after an order than most. Got a job for me, Mr. Ricks?"

"No, I haven't, Mr. Peck. I'm out of it, you know. Retired ten years ago. This office is merely a head-quarters for giving advice, rallying the troops and watching over the company carrying my name. Our Mr. Skinner is the chap you should see."

"I have seen Mr. Skinner, sir," the erstwhile warrior replied, "but he wasn't very sympathetic. He informed me that there wasn't sufficient business to keep his present staff of salesmen busy, no matter my experience, so then I told him I'd take anything, from stenographer up. I'm the champion one-handed typist of the United States Army. I can tally lumber and bill it. I can keep books and answer the telephone."

"No luck, eh?"

"No, sir. He said there's not a job to be found, much as he'd like to have one to offer."

"Well, now, son," Cappy informed his cheerful visitor confidentially, "you take my tip and see my son-in-law, Captain Matt Peasley. He's high, low and jack-in-the-game in the shipping end of our business."

"I have also interviewed with Captain Peasley. He was very kind. He said he felt he owed me a job, but business is so bad he couldn't make a place for me. He told me he is now carrying a dozen ex-service men merely because he hasn't the heart to let them go, even though he doesn't have enough work to go around. I believe him."

"Well, my dear Mr. Peck! Why do you come to me then?"

"Because," Mr. Peck replied smilingly, "I want you to go over their heads and give me a job. I don't care a hoot what it is, provided I can do it. If I can do it, I'll do it better than it was ever done before, and if I can't do that I'll quit to save you from having to fire me. I'm four years behind the procession and have to catch up. I have the best of references—"

"I see you have," Cappy cut in blandly, and pressed the push-button on his desk. Mr. Skinner entered. He glanced at William E. Peck and then turned inquiring eyes toward Cappy Ricks.

"Mr. Peck, will you excuse us for a moment?" Cappy asked brightly, gesturing Peck to the corridor. As soon as the door closed, Cappy set his eyes straight on his target. "Skinner," Cappy purred amiably, "I've been thinking over the proposition to send Andrews out to the Shanghai office, and I've come to this conclusion. We'll have to take a chance. At the present time that office is in the charge of a stenographer, and we've got to get a manager on the job without further loss of time. So I'll tell you what we'll do. We'll send Andrews out on the next boat, but inform him that his position is temporary. Then if he doesn't make good out there we can take him back into this office, where he is a most valuable man. Meanwhile—ahem! hum-m-m! Harumph!—meanwhile, you'd oblige me greatly, Skinner, if you would consent to take this young man into your office and give him a good work-out to see the stuff he's made of. As a favor to me, Skinner, as a favor to me."

Mr. Skinner, in the language of the sporting world, was down for the count—and knew it. If he had learned one thing from working with Cappy Ricks it was this: that the commanding general's request is always tantamount to an order.

"Very well, sir," Mr. Skinner replied wearily. "I imagine you've already offered him the job. Have you arranged the compensation to be given to Mr. Peck?"

Cappy threw up a deprecating hand. "That detail is entirely up to you, Skinner. Far be it from me to interfere in the internal administration of your department." Cappy turned to the door and ushered Mr. Peck back into his office. "Naturally you will pay Mr. Peck what he is worth and not a cent more." He turned to the triumphant Peck, who was beginning to understand that he had gotten the job. "Now, you listen to me, young feller. If you think you're slipping gracefully into a good thing, disabuse your mind of that impression right now. You'll step right up to the plate, and you'll hit the ball fairly on the nose and you'll do it early and often. The first time you tip a foul, you'll be warned. The second time you do it you'll get a week's lay-off to type up bills and think it over, and the third time you'll be out—for keeps. Do I make myself clear?"

"You do, sir," Mr. Peck declared happily. "All I ask is fighting room and I'll hack my way into membership among Mr. Skinner's most prized possessions. Thank you, Mr. Skinner, for consenting to take me on, especially in these times. I appreciate your action very, very much and shall endeavor to be worthy of your confidence."

"Young scoundrel! In-fer-nal young scoundrel!" Cappy murmured to himself. "He has a sense of humor! Ah, poor old by-the-book Skinner! Ever since the market broke he's been spooked and lost all his spark. If he ever gets a new or unconventional thought in his head, the electricity will kill him overnight. He's hopping mad right now, because he can't say a word in his own defense, but if he doesn't make hell look like a summer holiday for Mr. Bill Peck, I'm due to be mercifully chloroformed. Good gracious, how empty life would be if I couldn't butt in and raise a little riot every once in so often."

Young Mr. Peck had risen and was standing at attention. "When do I report for duty, sir?" he queried of Mr. Skinner.

"Whenever you're ready," Skinner retorted with a wintry smile. Mr. Peck glanced at a cheap wrist watch. "It's twelve o'clock now," he soliloquized aloud. "I'll pop out, wrap myself around some rations and report on the job at one P.M. I might just as well knock out half a day's pay." He glanced at Cappy Ricks and quoted:

Count that day lost whose low descending sun
Finds prices shot to glory and business done for
   fun.

Unable to maintain his composure in the face of such levity during office hours, Mr. Skinner withdrew, still wrapped in his sub-Antarctic dignity. As the door closed behind him, Mr. Peck's eyebrows went up in a manner indicative of apprehension.

"I'm off to a bad start, Mr. Ricks," he opined.

"You only asked for a start," Cappy piped back at him. "I didn't guarantee you a *good* start, and I wouldn't because I can't. I can only drive Skinner and Matt Peasley so far—and no farther. There's always a point at which I back down—er—ah—William."

"More familiarly known as *Bill* Peck, sir."

"Very well, Bill." Cappy slid out to the edge of his chair and peered at Bill Peck balefully over the top of his spectacles. "I'll have my eye on you, young feller," he shrilled. "I freely acknowledge our indebtedness to you, but the day you get the notion in your head that this office is a ride—" He paused thoughtfully. "I wonder what Skinner *will* pay you?" he mused. "Oh, well," he continued, "whatever it is, take it, and when the moment is propitious—and provided you've earned it—I'll intercede and get you a raise based on your time at Portland Lumber."

"Thank you very much, sir. You are most kind. Good-day, sir."

And Bill Peck picked up his hat and limped out of

The Presence. Scarcely had the door closed behind him than Mr. Skinner re-entered Cappy Ricks' lair. He opened his mouth to speak, but Cappy silenced him with an imperious finger.

"Not a peep out of you, Skinner," he chirped amiably. "I know exactly what you're going to say and I admit your right to say it, but—as—ahem! Harumph-h-h!—now, Skinner, listen to reason. How the devil could you have the head to turn away that go-getter lumber salesman and the heart to reject that wounded ex-soldier? There he stood, and on his face the grin of an unwhipped, unbeatable man. But you—blast your cold, unfeeling soul, Skinner!—looked him in the eye and turned him down like a drunkard turns down near-beer, simply because you haven't got a single go-getter tamping down a territory in the whole United States of America. Skinner, how *could* you do it?"

Undaunted by Cappy's admonitory finger, Mr. Skinner struck a distinctly defiant attitude.

"There is no sentiment in business," he replied angrily. "A week ago last Thursday the local posts of the American Legion commenced their organized drive for jobs for their wounded and unemployed, and within three days you've sawed off two hundred and nine such jobs on the various corporations that you control. You'd have hired them all if we hadn't stopped you. The gang you shipped up to the mill in Washington has already applied for a new post to be known as Cappy Ricks Post No. 534. We'll have to discharge experienced men to make room for any more ex-soldiers, and we're stretched too far," Skinner complained. "I tell you, sir, the Ricks interests have absorbed all the old soldiers possible and at the present moment those interests are overflowing with glory."

"Well, Mr. Peck is the last one I'll ask you to absorb, Skinner," Cappy promised contritely.

"To be frank, Mr. Ricks, Mr. Peck doesn't make a hit with me. He applied to me for a job and I gave him his answer. Then he went to Captain Matt and was refused; so, just to demonstrate his bad taste, he went over our heads and induced you to pitchfork him into a job. He'll curse the day he was inspired to do that."

"Skinner! Skinner! Look me in the eye! Do you know why I asked you to take on Bill Peck?"

"I do. Because you're too tender-hearted for your own good."

"You unimaginative dunderhead! How could I reject a man who simply would not be rejected? Why, I'll bet a ripe peach that Bill Peck was one of

the doggonedest finest soldiers you ever saw. He
carries his objective. He sized you up just like that,
Skinner. He declined to permit you to block him.
Skinner, that Peck person has been opposed by
experts. Yes, sir—experts! What kind of a job are
you going to give him?"

"Andrews' job, of course."

"Oh, yes, I forgot. Skinner, haven't we got about
half a million feet of skunk spruce to sell off?" Mr.
Skinner nodded and Cappy continued with all the
naïve eagerness of one who has just made a mar-
velous discovery, which he is confident will revolu-
tionize science. "Give him that stinking stuff to
peddle, Skinner, and if you can dig up a couple of
dozen carloads of red fir or bull pine in transit, or
some short or odd-length stock, or some larch ceil-
ing or flooring, or some hemlock random stock—in
fact, anything the trade doesn't want as a gift—you
get me, don't you, Skinner?"

Mr. Skinner smiled his swordfish smile. "And if
he fails to make good—*au revoir*, eh?"

"Yes, I suppose so, although I hate to think about
it. On the other hand, if he makes good he's to
have Andrews' current salary. We must be fair,
Skinner. Whatever our faults we must always be
fair." He rose and patted the general manager's lean

shoulder. "There, there, Skinner. Forgive me if I've been a trifle—ah—ahem!—precipitate and—er—harumph-h-h! Skinner, if you put a prohibitive price on that skunk fir, by the Holy Pink-toed Prophet, I'll fire you! Be fair, be fair. No dirty work. Remember, Mr. Peck has half of his left forearm buried in France."

# · III ·

AT TWELVE-THIRTY, AS CAPPY WAS HURRYING UP
California Street to luncheon at the Commercial
Club, he met Bill Peck limping down the sidewalk.
The ex-soldier stopped him and handed him a card.
"What do you think of that, sir?" he queried.
"Isn't it a neat business card?"
Cappy read:

RICKS LUMBER & LOGGING COMPANY
Lumber and its products
248 California St.,
San Francisco.
REPRESENTED BY WILLIAM E. PECK
*If you can drive nails in it—we have it!*

Cappy Ricks ran a speculative thumb over Bill Peck's business card. It was engraved. And copper plates or steel dies are not made in half an hour!

"By the Twelve Ragged Apostles!" This was Cappy's most terrible oath and he never employed it unless rocked to his very foundations. "Bill, as one bandit to another—come clean. When did you first make up your mind to go to work for us?"

"A week ago," Bill Peck replied blandly.

"Why Ricks Logging & Lumbering?"

"Because all my hustling for Portland Lumber could never catch up to your timber. You've got the best stock in the business."

"And what was your grade when the war ended?"

"I was a buck private."

"I don't believe you. Didn't anybody ever offer you something better?"

"Frequently. However, if I had accepted I would have had to resign the nicest job I ever had. There wasn't much money in it, but it was filled with excitement and interesting experiments. I used to disguise myself as a Christmas tree or a box car and pick off sharp-shooters. I was known as Peck's Bad Boy. I was often tempted to quit, but whenever I'd reflect on the number of American lives I was saving daily, a commission was just a scrap of paper to me."

"If you'd ever started in any other branch of the service you'd have run John J. Pershing down to lance corporal. Bill, listen! Have you ever had any experience selling skunk spruce?"

Bill Peck was plainly puzzled. He shook his head. "What sort of lumber is it?" he asked.

"Humboldt County, California, spruce, and it's coarse and stringy and wet and heavy and smells just like a skunk directly after using. I'm afraid Skinner's going to start you at the bottom—and skunk spruce is it."

"Can you drive nails in it, Mr. Ricks?"

"Oh, yes."

"Does anybody ever buy skunk spruce, sir?"

"Oh, occasionally one of our bright young salesmen digs up someone who's willing to try anything once. Otherwise, of course, we would not continue to manufacture it. Fortunately, Bill, we have very little of it, but whenever our woods boss runs across a tree he hasn't the heart to leave it standing and, as a result, we always have enough skunk spruce on hand to keep our salesmen humble."

"I can sell anything—at a price," Bill Peck replied, and continued on his way back to the office. "It shall be done."

# · IV ·

FOR TWO MONTHS CAPPY RICKS SAW NOTHING of Bill Peck. That enterprising veteran had been sent out into the Utah, Arizona, New Mexico and Texas territory the moment he had familiarized himself with the numerous details regarding freight rates, weights and the mills he represented, all things which a salesman should be familiar with before he starts out on the road. From Salt Lake City he wired an order for two carloads of larch rustic and in Ogden he managed to inveigle a retail yard with which Mr. Skinner had been trying to do business for years, into sampling a carload of skunk spruce boards, random lengths and grades, at a dollar above the price given him by Skinner. In

Arizona he worked up some new business in mining timbers, but it was not until he got into the heart of Texas that Comrade Peck really commenced to demonstrate his selling ability. Standard oil derricks were his specialty and he shot the orders in so fast that Mr. Skinner was forced to wire him for mercy and instruct him to devote his talent to the more commercially provident disposal of cedar shingles and siding, Douglas fir and redwood. Eventually he completed his circle and worked his way home, via Los Angeles, pausing however in the San Joaquin Valley to sell two more carloads of skunk spruce. When this order was wired in, Mr. Skinner came to Cappy Ricks with the telegram.

"Well, I must admit Bill Peck can sell lumber," he announced grudgingly. "He has secured five new accounts and here is an order for two more carloads of skunk spruce. I'll have to raise his salary about the first of the year."

"My dear Skinner, why the devil wait until the first of the year? Your pernicious habit of deferring the inevitable parting with money has cost us the services of more than one good man. You know you have to raise Bill Peck's salary sooner or later, so why not do it now and smile like a toothpaste advertisement while you're doing it? Bill Peck will feel a whole lot better as a result, and who knows? He may conclude you're a human being, after all, and learn to love you."

"Very well, sir. I'll give him the same salary Andrews was getting before Peck took over the territory."

"Skinner, you make it impossible for me to refrain from showing you who's boss around here. He's better than Andrews, isn't he?"

"I think he is, sir."

"Well then, for the love of a square deal, pay him more and pay it to him from the first day he went to work. Get out. You make me nervous. By the way, how is Andrews getting along in the Shanghai job?"

"He's helping the cable company pay its income tax. Cables about three times a week on matters he should decide for himself. Matt Peasley is disgusted with him."

"Ah! Well, I'm not disappointed. And I suppose Matt will be in here before long to remind me that I was the bright boy who picked Andrews for the job. Well, I did, but I call upon you to remember, Skinner, when I'm assailed, that Andrews' appointment was temporary."

"Yes, sir, it was."

"Well, I suppose I'll have to cast about for his

successor and beat Matt out of his cheap 'I told you so' triumph. I think Bill Peck has some of the earmarks of a good manager for our Shanghai office, but I'll have to test him a little further." He looked up humorously at Mr. Skinner. "Skinner, my dear boy," he continued, "I'm going to have him deliver a blue vase."

Mr. Skinner's cold features actually glowed. "Well, tip the chief of police and the proprietor of the store off this time and save yourself some money," he warned Cappy. "I don't envy Mr. Peck, and I have every hope that he'll give you less of a tangle than the rest of us." He walked to the window and looked down into California Street. He continued to smile.

"Yes," Cappy continued dreamily, "You'll agree with me, Skinner, that if he delivers the blue vase he'll be worth ten thousand dollars a year as our Asia manager?"

"I'll say he will." Mr. Skinner replied slangily.

"Very well, then. Arrange matters, Skinner, so that he will be available for me at one o'clock, a week from Sunday. I'll attend to the other details."

Mr. Skinner nodded. He was still chuckling when he departed for his own office.

# · V ·

A WEEK FROM THE SUCCEEDING SATURDAY, MR. Skinner did not come down to the office, but a telephone message from his home informed the chief clerk that Mr. Skinner was at home and somewhat indisposed. The chief clerk was to advise Mr. Peck that he, Mr. Skinner, had contemplated having a conference with the latter that day, but that his indisposition would prevent this. Mr. Skinner hoped to be feeling much better tomorrow, and since he was very desirous of a conference with Mr. Peck before the latter should depart on his next selling pilgrimage, on Monday, would Mr. Peck be good enough to call at Mr. Skinner's house at one o'clock on Sunday afternoon? Mr. Peck sent back word that he would be there at the appointed time and was rewarded with Mr. Skinner's thanks, via the chief clerk.

Promptly at one o'clock the following day, Bill Peck reported at the general manager's house. He found Mr. Skinner in bed, reading the paper and looking surprisingly well. He trusted Mr. Skinner felt better than he looked. Mr. Skinner did, and at once entered into a discussion of the new customers, other prospects he particularly desired Mr. Peck to approach, new business to be investigated and further details without end. And in the midst of this conference Cappy Ricks telephoned.

A portable telephone stood on a commode beside Mr. Skinner's bed, so the latter answered immediately. Mr. Peck watched Skinner listen attentively for fully two minutes, then heard him say:

"Mr. Ricks, I'm terribly sorry. I'd love to do this errand for you, but really I'm under the weather. In fact, I'm in bed as I speak to you now. But Mr. Peck is here with me and I'm sure he'll be very happy to attend to the matter for you."

"By all means," Bill Peck hastened to assure the general manager. "Who does Mr. Ricks want killed and where will he have the body delivered?"

"Hah-hah! Hah-hah!" Mr. Skinner had a singularly annoying, mirthless laugh, as if he begrudged himself such an unheard-of indulgence. "Mr. Peck says," he informed Cappy, "that he'll be delighted to attend to the matter for you. He wants to know whom you want killed and where you wish the body delivered. Hah-hah! Hah! Peck, Mr. Ricks will speak to you."

Bill Peck took the telephone. "Good afternoon, Mr. Ricks."

"Hello, old soldier. What are you doing this afternoon?"

"Final preparations for my sales trip tomorrow—after I conclude my conference with Mr. Skinner. Most everything is pulled together, but there are a few things that I'd like to put in order before I hit the road. By the way, he has just given me a most handsome boost in salary, for which I am most appreciative. I feel, however, that in addition to Mr. Skinner's graciousness, you have put in a kind word for me with him, and I want to thank you—"

"Tut, tut. Not a peep out of you, sir. Not a peep. You get nothing for nothing from Skinner or me. However, in view of the fact that you're feeling kindly toward me this afternoon, I wish you'd put aside your things for a few minutes and do a little errand for me. I hate to make a messenger out of you—er—ah—ahem! That is—harumph-h-h—!"

"I have no false pride, Mr. Ricks."

"Thank you, Bill. Glad you feel that way about it. Bill, I was prowling around town this forenoon, after church, and down in a store on Sutter Street, between Stockton and Powell Street, on the right hand side as you face Market Street, I saw a blue vase in a window. I have a weakness for vases, Bill. I'm sharp on them, too. Now, this vase I saw isn't very expensive as vases go—in fact, I wouldn't buy it for my collection—but one of my dear friends has the mate to that blue vase I saw in the window, and I know she'd be prouder than Punch if she had two of them—one for each side of her drawing room mantel, understand?

"Now, I'm leaving from the Southern Pacific depot at eight o'clock tonight, bound for Santa Barbara to attend her wedding anniversary tomorrow. I forget what anniversary it is, Bill, but I have been informed by my daughter that this crazy little blue vase just fills the order. Understand?"

"Yes, sir. You feel that it would be most graceful on your part if you could bring this little blue vase down to Santa Barbara with you tonight. You have to have it tonight, because if you wait until the store opens on Monday the vase will reach your hostess twenty-four hours after her anniversary party."

"Exactly, Bill. Now, I've simply got to have that vase. If I had discovered it yesterday I wouldn't be asking you to get it for me today, Bill. But I've got to finish up some cables for our manager in the Shanghai office, and I don't see where I can find the time to do both."

"Please do not make any explanations or apologies, Mr. Ricks. You have described the vase—no you haven't. What sort of blue is it, how tall is it and what is, approximately, its greatest diameter? Does it set on a base or does it not? Is it a solid blue, or is it figured?"

"It's a Cloisonné vase, Bill—sort of old Dutch blue, or Delft, with some Chinese or Japanese doodads on it. I couldn't describe it exactly, but it has some birds and flowers on it. It's about a foot tall and four inches in diameter and sets on a teak-wood base."

"Very well, sir. You shall have it."

"And you'll deliver it to me in stateroom A, car seven, aboard the train at Third and Townsend Streets, at seven fifty-five tonight?"

"Yes, sir."

"Thank you, Bill. The expense will be trifling, I do know that. Collect it from the cashier in the morning, and tell him to charge it to my account." And Cappy hung up.

At once Mr. Skinner took up the thread of the interrupted conference, and it was not until three o'clock that Bill Peck left his house and proceeded downtown to locate Cappy Ricks's blue vase.

Along his way, he remembered the stack of papers waiting on his desk before his trip. He had promised Mr. Skinner a few short hours earlier that he would file them on their way before he left, despite the cold man's insistence that they might wait. "I wonder if there's anyone down at Ricks Logging & Lumbering that could take on one or the other," the young man mused, but then recalled that he'd given both Cappy Ricks and Mr. Skinner his personal word. He was the man to get both jobs done.

He proceeded to the block in Sutter Street between Stockton and Powell Streets, and although he walked patiently up one side of the street and down the other, not a single vase of any description showed in any window, nor could he find a single shop where such a vase as Cappy had described might, perchance, be displayed for sale.

"I think the old boy has erred in the co-ordinates

of the target," Bill Peck concluded, "or else I misunderstood him. I'll telephone his house and ask him to repeat them."

He did, but nobody was at home except a butler, and all he knew was that Mr. Ricks was out and the hour of his return was unknown. He tried the telephone at the office, to no avail. So Mr. Peck went back to Sutter Street and scoured once more every shop window in the block. Then he scouted two blocks above Powell and two blocks below Stockton. Still the blue vase remained invisible.

So he transferred his search to a corresponding area on Bush Street, and when that failed, he went painstakingly over four blocks of Post Street. He was without results when he moved one block further west and one further south and discovered the blue vase in a huge plate-glass window of a shop on Geary Street near Grant Avenue. He surveyed it critically and was convinced that it was the object he sought.

He tried the door, but it was locked, as he had anticipated it would be. So he kicked the door and raised a racket, hoping against hope that the noise might bring a watchman from the rear of the building. In vain. He backed out to the edge of the sidewalk and read the sign over the door:

## B. Johnson's Art Shop

This was a start, so Mr. Peck limped over to the Palace Hotel and procured a telephone directory. By actual count there were nineteen B. Johnsons scattered throughout the city, so before commencing to call the nineteen, Bill Peck borrowed the city directory from the hotel clerk and scanned it for the particular B. Johnson who owned the art shop. His search availed him nothing. B. Johnson was listed as an art dealer at the address where the blue vase reposed in the shop window. That was all.

"I suppose he's a commuter," Mr. Peck concluded, and at once proceeded to procure directories of the adjacent cities of Berkeley, Oakland, and Alameda. They were not available, so in despair he changed a dollar into five cent pieces, sought a telephone booth and commenced calling up all the B. Johnsons in San Francisco. Of the nineteen, four did not answer, three were temporarily disconnected, six replied in languages he couldn't decipher, five were not the B. Johnson he sought and one swore that his name was actually Jolson and it was about time the telephone directory got it right.

The B. Johnsons resident in Berkeley, Oakland, Alameda, San Rafael, Sausalito, Mill Valley, San

Mateo, Redwood City and Palo Alto were next telephoned to, and when this long and expensive task was done, Ex-private Bill Peck emerged from the telephone booth wringing wet with perspiration and as irritable as a clucking hen. Once outside the hotel he raised his haggard face to heaven and dumbly queried of the Almighty what He meant by saving him from quick death on the field of honor only to condemn him to be talked to death by B. Johnsons in civil life.

It was now six o'clock. Suddenly Peck had an inspiration. Was the name spelled Johnson, Johnsen, Jonson, Jansen or Jonsen?

"If I have to take a city census again tonight I'll die," he told himself desperately, and went back to the art shop.

The sign read:

*B. Jonson's Art Shop*

"I wish I knew a bootlegger's joint," poor Peck complained. "I'm pretty far gone and a little wood alcohol couldn't hurt me much now. Why, I could have sworn it was spelled with an H. It seems to me I noted that particularly."

He went back to the hotel telephone booth and

commenced calling up all the B. Jonsons in town. There were eight of them and six of them were out, one was maudlin with liquor and the other was very deaf and shouted unintelligibly.

"Peace hath its barbarities no less than war," Mr. Peck sighed. He changed a twenty-dollar bill into nickles, dimes and quarters, returned to the hot, ill-smelling telephone booth and proceed to lay down a barrage of telephone calls to the B. Jonsons of all towns of any importance contiguous to San Francisco Bay. And he was lucky. On the sixth call he located the particular B. Jonson in San Rafael, only to be informed by B. Jonson's cook that Mr. Jonson was dining at the home of a Mr. Simons in Mill Valley.

There were three Mr. Simons in Mill Valley, and Peck called them all before connecting with the right one. Yes, Mr. B. Jonson was there. Who wished to speak to him? Mr. Heck? Oh, Mr. Lake! A silence. Then—"Mr. Jonson says he doesn't know any Mr. Lake and wants to know the nature of your business. He is dining and doesn't like to be disturbed unless the matter is of grave importance."

"Tell him Mr. Peck wishes to speak to him on a matter of very great importance," wailed the private.

"Mr. Metz? Mr. Ben Metz?"

"No, no, no. Peck—P-e-c-k."

"D-e-c-k?"

"No, P."

"C?"

"P."

"Oh, yes, E. E—what?"

"C-k—"

"Oh, yes, Mr. Eckstein."

"Call Jonson to the phone or I'll go over there on the next boat and tell him you're the person who wouldn't get him to the phone when I called to tell him his store is on fire."

That message was evidently delivered for almost instantly Mr. B. Jonson was puffing and spluttering into the phone.

"Is this—the—fire—marshal?" he managed to articulate.

"Listen, Mr. Jonson. Your store is not on fire, but I had to say so in order to get you to the telephone, for which I apologize. I am Mr. Peck, a total stranger to you. You have a blue vase in your shop on Geary Street in San Francisco. I need to buy it and I need to buy it before seven forty-five tonight. What do I need to do for you to come across the bay and open the store and sell me that vase?"

"Such an emergency! Do you think I am crazy?"

"No, Mr. Jonson, I do not. I'm the only crazy man talking. I'm crazy for that vase and I've got to have it right away."

"You know how much that vase costs?" Mr. B. Jonson's voice dripped syrup.

"No, and I don't give a hoot what it costs. I want what I want when I want it. Do I get it?"

"Well, lemme see. What time is it?" A silence while B. Jonson evidently looked at his watch. "It is now a quarter of seven, Mr. Eckstein, and the next train from Mill Valley doesn't leave until eight o'clock. That will get me to San Francisco at eight-fifty—and I am dining with my friends and I have just finished my soup."

"It will be worth your effort, Mr. Jonson. I want that blue vase."

"Well, I tell you, Mr. Eckstein, if you have to have it, call up my head salesman, Herman Joost, in the Chilton Apartments—Prospect three-two-four-nine, and tell him I said he should come down right away and sell you that blue vase. If he needs to, he can call me here. Good-bye, Mr. Eckstein."

And B. Jonson hung up.

Instantly Peck called Prospect 3249 and asked for

Herman Joost. Mr. Joost's mother answered. She was sorry because Herman was not at home, but vouchsafed the information that he was dining at the country club. Which country club? She did not know. So Peck procured from the hotel clerk a list of the country clubs in and around San Francisco and started calling them up. At eight o'clock he was still being informed that Mr. Juice was not a member, that Mr. Luce wasn't in, that Mr. Coos had been dead three months and that Mr. Boos had played but eight holes when he received a telegram calling him back to New York. At the other clubs Mr. Joust was unknown.

"Licked," murmured Bill Peck, "but never let it be said that I didn't go down fighting. I'm going to heave a brick through that show window, leave a note and get the vase to Mr. Ricks if it kills me. I owe it to him."

He engaged a taxicab and instructed the driver to wait for him at the corner of Geary and Stockton Streets. Also, he borrowed from the chauffeur a ball-peen hammer. When he reached the art shop of B. Jonson, however, a policeman was standing in the doorway, violating the general orders of a policeman on duty by surreptitiously smoking a cigar.

"Better that he's there, since now I don't have the temptation to crack that window," the desperate Peck decided, and continued on down the street, crossed to the other side and came back, thinking about the choices that lay before him. It was now dark and over the art shop B. Jonson's name burned in small red, white and blue electric lights.

And lo, it was spelled B. Johnson!

Ex-private William E. Peck sat down on a fire hydrant and cursed with rage. His weak leg hurt him, too, and for some damnable reason, the stump of his left arm developed the feeling that his missing hand was itchy. It dawned on him that it was itchy for the paperwork back at Ricks Logging & Lumbering Company.

"The world is filled with obstacles," he raved furiously. "I'm tired and I'm hungry. I skipped luncheon and I've been too busy to think of dinner. And I've caught myself in two failed duties that I can't recover from."

He walked back to his taxicab and went to the office where, hope springing eternal in his breast, he picked up his papers while calling Prospect 3249 again and discovered that the missing Herman Joost had returned to the bosom of his family. To him the frantic Peck delivered the message of B. Jonson, whereupon the cautious Herman Joost replied that he would confirm the authenticity of the message by telephoning to Mr. Jonson at Mr. Simon's home in Mill Valley. If Mr. B. Jonson or Johnson confirmed Mr. Kek's story he, the said Herman Joost would be at the store sometime before nine o'clock, and if Mr. Kek cared to, he might await him there.

Mr. Kek said he would be delighted to wait for him there. He knew just what he'd do to kill the time.

At nine-fifteen Herman Joost appeared on the scene. On his way down the street he had taken the precaution to pick up a policeman and bring him along with him. The lights were switched on in the store and Mr. Joost lovingly extracted the blue vase from the window.

"What's the cursed thing worth?" Peck enquired.

"Two thousand dollars," Mr. Joost replied without so much as the quiver of an eyelash. "Cash," he added, apparently as an afterthought.

The exhausted Peck leaned against the sturdy guardian of the law and sighed. This was the final straw. He had about ten dollars in his possession and ages until the next set of bankers' hours.

"You refuse, absolutely, to accept my check?" he quavered.

"I don't know you, Mr. Peck," Herman Joost replied simply.

"Where's your telephone?"

Mr. Joost led Peck to the telephone and the latter called up Mr. Skinner.

"Mr. Skinner," he announced, "this is all that is mortal of Bill Peck speaking. I've got the store open and for two thousand dollars—cash—I can buy the blue vase Mr. Ricks has set his heart upon."

"Oh, Peck, dear fellow," Mr. Skinner purred sympathetically. "Have you been all this time on that errand? I hope you finished up your work before—"

"I have. And I did. And I'm going to stick to this job until I deliver the goods. Could you bring the two thousand dollars down to me at B. Johnson's Art Shop on Geary Street near Grant Avenue? I'm too utterly exhausted to go up for it."

"My dear Mr. Peck, I haven't two thousand dollars in my house. That is too great a sum of money to keep on hand."

"Well, then, come downtown, open up the office safe and release the money to me on Mr. Ricks' behalf."

"Time lock on the office safe, Peck. Impossible."

"Well then, come downtown and identify me at

hotels and cafes and restaurants so I can cash my own check."

"Is your check good, Mr. Peck?"

The flood of invective which had been accumulating in Mr. Peck's system all the afternoon was now ready to break its bounds. He wanted to scream at Mr. Skinner a blasphemous invitation to betake himself to the lower regions.

"Tomorrow morning," he promised hoarsely, "I'll show you what a miserable, cold-blooded, untrusting slacker you are. Now, I've got other matters to tackle." He excused himself, and hung up the phone with a slam.

He called up Cappy Ricks' residence next, and asked for Captain Matt Peasley, who, he knew, made his home with his father-in-law. Matt Peasley came to the telephone and listened sympathetically to Peck's tale of woe.

"Peck, that's the worst outrage I ever heard of," he declared. "The idea of setting you such a task. You take my advice and forget the blue vase."

"I can't," Peck panted. "Mr. Ricks will feel mighty chagrined if I fail to get the vase to him. I wouldn't disappoint him for my right arm. He's been a dead game sport with me, Captain Peasley."

"But it's too late to get the vase to him, Peck. He

left the city at eight o'clock and it is now almost half past nine."

"I know, but if I can secure legal possession of the vase I'll get it to him before he leaves the train at Santa Barbara at six o'clock tomorrow morning."

"How?"

"There's a flying school out at the Marina and one of the pilots there is a friend of mine. He'll fly to Santa Barbara with me and the vase."

"You're crazy," Peasley said admiringly.

"I know it. Please lend me two thousand dollars."

"What for?"

"To pay for the vase."

"Now I know you're crazy—or drunk. Why if Cappy Ricks ever forgot himself to the extent of paying two hundred dollars for a vase he'd bleed to death in an hour."

"Won't you let me have two thousand dollars, Captain Peasley?"

"I will not, Peck, my friend. Go home and to bed and know you did your best. You've done more than enough."

"Please. You can cash your checks. You're known so much better than I, and it's Sunday night—"

"And it's a fine way to disturb my one evening of quiet," Matt Peasley retorted and hung up.

"Well," Herman Joost queried, "do we stay here all night?"

Bill Peck bowed his head. "Look here," he demanded suddenly, "do you know a good diamond when you see it?"

"I do," Herman Joost replied.

"Will you wait here until I go to my hotel and get one?"

"Sure."

Bill Peck limped painfully away. Forty minutes later he returned with a platinum ring set with diamonds and sapphires.

"What are they worth?" he demanded.

Herman Joost looked the ring over lovingly and appraised it conservatively at twenty-five hundred dollars.

"Take it as security for the payment of my check," Peck pleaded. "Give me a receipt for it and after my check has gone through clearing I'll come back and get the ring."

Fifteen minutes later, with the blue vase packed in excelsior and reposing in a stout cardboard box, Bill Peck entered a restaurant and ordered dinner. When he had dined he engaged a taxi, stopped by the office to file his reports on new opportunities for selling skunk wood in other territories and was driven to the flying field at the Marina. From the night watchman he ascertained the address of his pilot friend and at midnight, with his friend at the wheel, Bill Peck and his blue vase soared up into the moonlight and headed south.

An hour and a half later they landed in a stubble field in the Salinas Valley and, bidding his friend good-bye, Bill Peck trudged across to the railroad track and sat down. When the train bearing Cappy Ricks came roaring down the valley, Peck twisted a Sunday paper with which he had provided himself into an improvised torch, which he lighted. Standing between the rails he swung the flaming paper frantically.

The train slid to a halt, a brakeman opened a vestibule door and Bill Peck stepped wearily aboard.

"What do you mean by flagging this train?" the brakeman demanded angrily, as he signaled the engineer to proceed. "Got a ticket?"

"No, but I've got the money to pay my way. And I flagged this train because I wanted to change my method of travel. I'm looking for a man in state-room A of car seven, and there's no way you can block me."

"Are you looking for that little old man with the Henry Clay collar and the white mutton-chop whiskers?"

"I certainly am."

"Well, he must have been looking for you just before we left San Francisco. He asked me if I had seen a one-armed man with a box under his good arm. I'll lead you to him."

A prolonged ringing at Cappy's stateroom door brought the old gentleman to the entrance in his nightshirt.

"Very sorry to have to disturb you, Mr. Ricks," said Bill Peck, "but the fact is there were so many Johnstons and Jonsons and Jolsons, and it was such a job to dig up two thousand dollars, that I failed to connect with you at seven fifty-five last night, as per orders. It was absolutely impossible for me to accomplish the task within the time limit set, but I was resolved that you should not be disappointed. Here is the vase. The shop wasn't within four blocks of where you thought it was, sir, but I'm sure I found the right one. It ought to be. It cost enough and was hard enough to get, so it should be precious enough to form a gift for any friend of yours."

Cappy Ricks stared at Bill Peck as if the latter were a wraith.

"By the Twelve Ragged Apostles!" he murmured. "By the Holy Pink-toed Prophet! We
changed the sign on you and we stacked the Johnsons on you and we set a policeman to guard the
shop to keep you from breaking the window, and
we made you dig up two thousand dollars on Sunday night in a town where you are practically
unknown, and while you missed the train at eight
o'clock, you overtake it at two o'clock in the morning and deliver the blue vase. Come in and rest
your poor old game leg, Bill. Brakeman, I'm much
obliged to you."

Bill Peck entered and slumped wearily down on
the settee. "So it was a plant?" he cracked, and his
voice trembled with rage. "Well, sir, you're an old
man and you've been good to me, so I do not
begrudge you your little joke, but Mr. Ricks, I can't
understand what would drive a decent person to put
someone through that. My leg hurts and my stump
hurts and my heart hurts—"

He paused, choking, and the tears of impotent
rage filled his eyes. "You shouldn't treat me that
way, sir," he complained presently. "I've been
trained to deliver on my promises, even when they
seem utterly foolish to me in hindsight; I've been

trained to satisfy them—on time, if possible, but if impossible, to satisfy them anyhow. I've been taught loyalty to my chief—and I'm sorry my chief found it necessary to send me on a goose chase for his own amusement. I haven't had a very good time the past three years and—when—when—you finally took me on I thought that this was my ch-ch-chance and—and—you can—pa-pa-pass your skunk spruce and larch rustic and short odd length stock to some slacker like Skinner—now that he's got my plan he's got a chance to make it—if—if—you don't have—to replace—Skinner, because he's cold—enough to—leave any man—out on the street—including—you—sir—"

Cappy Ricks held Bill Peck's aching eyes with his own.

"Bill, it was cruel—damnably cruel, but I had a big job for you and I had to find out a lot of things about you before I entrusted you with that job. So I arranged to give you the Degree of the Blue Vase, which is the supreme test of a go-getter. It's a job that many before you have handed off to one of the messengers at the office, thinking that it was beneath them. It's a job that many before you have walked away from at the first sign of an obstacle.

You thought you carried into this stateroom a two thousand dollar vase, but between ourselves, what you really carried in was a ten thousand dollar job as our Shanghai manager."

"Wha-what!"

"Every time I have to pick out a permanent holder of a job worth ten thousand dollars, or more, I give the candidate the Degree of the Blue Vase," Cappy explained. "I've had three men out of a field of thirty deliver the vase, Bill. I'm sure you can guess who two of them are, and why they gave you the advice they did today, as cruel as it may have seemed at the time."

Bill Peck had forgotten his rage, but the tears of his recent fury still glistened in his bold blue eyes. "Thank you, sir. I'll make good in Shanghai."

"I know you will, Bill. Now tell me, weren't you tempted to quit when you discovered the almost insuperable obstacles placed in your way?"

"Yes, sir, I was. I wanted to commit suicide before I'd finished telephoning all the J-o-h-n-s-o-n-s in the world. And when I started on the J-o-n-s-o-n-s— well, it's this way, sir. I just couldn't quit because that would have been disloyal to a man I once knew."

"Who was he?" Cappy demanded, and there was awe in his voice.

"He was my brigadier, and he had a brigade motto: It shall be done. When the divisional commander called him up and told him to move forward with his brigade and occupy certain territory, our brigadier would say: 'Very well, sir. It shall be done.' If any officer in his brigade showed signs of flunking his job because it appeared impossible, the brigadier would just look at him once—and then that officer would remember the motto and go and do his job or die trying.

"In the army, sir, the *esprit de corps* doesn't bubble up from the bottom. It filters down from the top. An organization is what its commanding officer is—neither better nor worse. In my company, when the top sergeant handed out a week of kitchen police to a buck, that buck was out of luck if he couldn't muster a grin and say: 'All right, sergeant. It shall be done.'

"The brigadier sent for me once and ordered me to go out and get a certain German sniper. I'd been pretty lucky—some days I got enough for a mess—and he'd heard of me. He opened a map and said to me: 'Here's about where he holes up. Go get him,

Private Peck.' Well, Mr. Ricks, I snapped into it and gave him a rifle salute, and said, 'Sir, it shall be done'—and I'll never forget the look that man gave me. He came down to the field hospital to see me after I'd walked into one of those Austrian 88's. I knew my left arm was a total loss and I suspected my left leg was about to leave me, and I was downhearted and wanted to die. He came and bucked me up. He said: 'Why, Private Peck, you aren't half dead. In civil life you're going to be worth half a dozen live ones—aren't you?' But I was pretty far gone and I told him I didn't believe it, so he gave me a hard look and said: 'Private Peck will do his utmost to recover and as a starter he will smile.' Of course, putting it in the form of an order, I had to give him the usual reply, so I grinned and said: 'Sir, it shall be done.' He was quite a man, sir, and his brigade had a soul—his soul—"

"I see, Bill. His soul goes marching on, eh, though now you're the commanding officer of your life. Who was he, Bill?"

Bill Peck named his idol.

"By the Twelve Ragged Apostles!" There was awe in Cappy Ricks' voice, there was reverence in his faded old eyes. "Son," he continued gently, "twenty-five years ago your brigadier was a candidate for an important job in my employ—and I gave him the Degree of the Blue Vase. He couldn't get the vase legitimately, so he threw a cobble-stone through the window, grabbed the vase and ran a mile and a half before the police captured him. Cost me a lot of money to square the case and keep it quiet. But he was too good, Bill, and I couldn't stand in his way; I let him go forward to his destiny. But tell me, Bill. How did you get the two thousand dollars to pay for this vase?"

"Once," said Ex-private Peck thoughtfully, "the brigadier and I were first at a dug-out entrance. It was a headquarters dug-out and they wouldn't surrender so I bombed them and then we went down. I found a finger with a ring on it—and the brigadier said if I didn't take the ring somebody else would. I left that ring as security for my check."

"But how could you have the courage to let me in for a two thousand dollar vase? Didn't you realize that the price was absurd and that I might repudiate the transaction?"

"Certainly not. You are responsible for the acts of your servant. You are a true blue sport and would never repudiate my action. You told me what to do, but you did not insult my intelligence by telling me how to do it. When my late brigadier sent me after the German sniper he didn't take into consideration the probability that the sniper might get me. He told me to get the sniper. It was my business to see to it that I accomplished my mission and carried my objective, which, of course, I could not have done if I had permitted the German to get me."

"I see, Bill. Well, if you don't want to see that blue vase again, give it to the porter in the morning. I paid fifteen cents for it in a five, ten and fifteen cent store. Meanwhile, hop into that upper berth and help yourself to a well-earned rest."

"But aren't you going to a wedding anniversary at Santa Barbara, Mr. Ricks?"

"I am not. Bill, I discovered a long time ago that it's a good idea for me to get out of town and play golf as often as I can. Besides which, prudence dictates that I remain away from the office for a week after the seeker of blue vases fails to deliver the goods and—by the way, Bill, what sort of a game do you play? Oh, forgive me. I forgot about your left arm."

"Say, look here, sir," Bill Peck retorted, "I'm big

enough and cocky enough to play one-handed golf."

"But, have you ever tried it?"

"No, sir," Bill Peck replied seriously, "but—it shall be done!"

# Skunk Project or Blue Vase

BILL PECK'S APPRENTICESHIP AT RICKS LOGGING & Lumbering Company offers lessons on developing a leadership attitude and image, building loyalty among the people who are setting your quotas and watching your performance, and communicating your readiness to take the next step in your career. In those first weeks out West, Bill didn't just meet his quota; he beat his quota. He didn't just sneak skunk wood into sales at the scheduled price; he found out how skunk wood could be invaluable to his customers. Your first few weeks or months in a new job or new position set the tone for your manager's expectations. You can choose to let them expect that you'll over-promise and under-deliver;

you can choose to let them expect that you'll hit their deadlines and targets; or you can choose to let them expect you'll over-promise *and* over-deliver. You never know when you'll get the test of the blue vase, but you should treat *every* project as though it is the blue vase—or your ticket to one.

## WATCHING OUT FOR HENDERSON

What's the difference between a Henderson and a Peck? What allows someone to make the leap from being a great follower to being a great manager and leader? Henderson and Peck are both great salesmen—the best Ricks Logging & Lumbering Company has seen in the course of several years, through good markets and bad. Yet Cappy knew that Henderson didn't have what it takes to run the show. The difference comes down to fulfilling the letter of an assignment versus filling the spirit of one. When you're working on a project or selling to a new customer, do you stick to the quotas and tactics that are handed to you, or do you try to find better, more productive, more efficient, and, possibly, more successful ways to get the job done? Do you draw on your own ideas and creativity to improve on your assignments—without being asked? Do you make decisions on your own, based on your training and experience, rather than turn to a supervisor? Bill Peck's go-getter attitude is based on his belief that he brings something to his work that transcends the rules, responsibilities, and tasks that he's been given. Henderson works to meet his job description; Peck works to exceed it.

## COURAGE OR EXPERIENCE

Cappy asks one question about Andrews and his ability to take on the Asian operations for Ricks Logging & Lumbering: "Does he have the courage?" Why? Not simply because he puts a premium on courage over experience; he assumes that anyone who might be up for the job has to have the experience needed. Courage, on the other hand, doesn't come with education or age, though it can be learned. Cappy is looking for courage because it speaks to confidence, commitment, enthusiasm— all of which go part and parcel with the go-getters of the world. While technologies have changed, no employer wants to be burdened by the modern equivalent of trans-Pacific telegrams, which speak

PETER B. KYNE

to ineffectual management. Leaders—whether managers or front-line workers—make decisions every
day, and decisions require courage: a belief in
your reasoning and your experience, as well as
the ability to stand by the decisions once they're
made.


## Opening Doors

Is it a coincidence that Bill Peck served in the same
squadron as Cappy Ricks? Or that he knows more
about Ricks's business than some of Ricks's own
employees? Of course not. A true go-getter uses
research to open doors. What gets under the skin of
the person you're trying to meet? Is it a competitor
who's muscling in on a territory or a sentimental
attachment to an alma mater, a charity, or a home-
town? What can you use to get past the people who
are guarding the gates so that you can give your
pitch—for a job or for a sale—directly to the person who can or will make the decision? In Peck's
case, he's done enough homework to know that
being a war veteran might help him with Cappy
Ricks—but the thing that will really grab him by
the throat, before he walks in the door, is informa-

tion about how to win in the timber game. Even once you're sitting across the table from someone, you'll have several more doors to open, so you need to have more than one key to make your meeting a success.

## THE LANGUAGE OF THE LINE

We can sometimes forget that so much of selling— our products and ourselves—is about that pull to the heartstrings, the connections we forge with other people based on shared values and shared experiences that come across in a momentary phrase dropped in conversation and not from a perfectly scripted pitch. Here, it's Cappy that's sold himself to Bill Peck, in an interesting twist of story-telling—in just one line, he's convinced Peck that not only will he give him a job, he'll give him an opportunity to prove himself. Selling goes both ways: it's a contract after all, whether for timber or for a career, and you should be looking for customers and employers who will fulfill their ends of the obligation with resourcefulness, honesty, and heart. Not only will you gain a great account or a great boss, you'll be more likely to build a long-term relationship that will take you much farther than you can realize. Keep an ear out for these moments.

## LOYALTY ON THE FRONT LINE

Bill Peck learned the importance of promises on the battleground, when the risks are high, the uncertainty great, and the hardships severe. Battle is probably the only leadership environment in which both followers and leaders would rather be somewhere else, but, unfortunately, business can often feel remarkably like a battle. Successful combat leaders help those they lead to perform at almost superhuman levels of productivity—but it's not just the leaders who are responsible for pulling through a battle. Everyone on the front lines has to be willing to put their lives at risk for others and for a cause; loyalty is a vital ingredient in keeping your calm, keeping your focus, and keeping your wits. Unsure how to react in a difficult, incredible situation? If you can be loyal to your values, to your goals, and—ideally—to the person you're reporting to, you'll have a compass for even the worst situations. Even when you don't have someone to inspire you day by day, you can turn to mentors from your past—a trusted teacher, the person who gave you your first shot in business—for literal or figurative support. What would he or she tell you to do? Be loyal to the lessons that started you on the road of life and career.

## THREE STRIKES

Every boss keeps a mental tally of your successes and your failures; you should too. Too bad that we can't balance them one for one—or keep the balance in our favor by a slight margin. Three strikes is usually all it takes to lose someone's confidence and trust, whether your supervisor's, your customers', your colleagues', or your own. It's impossible to keep track of your strikes unless you know, exactly, what counts as a strike and what counts as a foul. Find out from your supervisor and your customers what they consider non-negotiable; and know what you, yourself, would consider such a personal failure that it would completely undermine your confidence and your go-getter spirit. Be honest with yourself when you tally up the hits, fouls, and strikes, but be careful not to let one strike—or even two—destroy an otherwise strong batting record.

## Reporting for Duty

How many of us would have the gumption to print up business cards for a job we hadn't landed? Bill Peck proves exactly how much of a go-getter he is by doing just that. Though it's not advice to take literally, Peck's gambit says a lot about imagining yourself succeeding before you've stepped in the door for the interview or the sales pitch, and about being ready to take an opportunity the moment it appears. Be prepared to deliver earlier than they're hoping, to start sooner than they're expecting, to prove your enthusiasm, your commitment, and your forethought by planning ahead for success. Make up your mind before the call that you're going to come out on the other end a winner, and know what you'll want to have on hand the moment you do. Go-getters are not marked by hesitation, dragged feet, or lowered goals.

## Pitchforking and Blocks

There's always a danger when you decide to pitchfork yourself over gatekeepers or lower-level decision-makers, as Bill Peck does when he goes straight to Cappy Ricks for a job. That's especially true when you've already been turned down by the very people you're trying to get past; doubly so if, like Mr. Skinner, they bring a whiff of bitterness to their business. The first rule of the go-getter is to never take "no" for an answer. But, in hunting for that eventual "yes" you need to play your cards right. How can you get around these blocks without starting out on the wrong foot? First, make sure that the person who will give you that "yes" really wields the power and influence you need to get past the Skinners of the world. It doesn't do you any good to succeed with someone who will only get vetoed or steamrolled. Second, like Peck, don't take "yes" for granted. Remember, every "yes" is an opportunity, not a gift.

## Skunk Wood and Odd Lengths

It usually seems as though the worst projects land on our laps just when we're trying to prove ourselves. Like Bill Peck, however, find the hook on which you can turn a disaster, an orphaned project, or a thankless task into your second success. What *can* be done with your skunk wood? If you can drive a nail into it, you can make your name selling it. Peck never forgets to realize that it's his job to sell the skunk wood, and therefore it's his job to find a way to do it. Does he have to show them himself that you can drive a nail into it? He'll show them. Does he have to show them himself how it can work just as well as timber that their competitors are selling them? He'll show them. Does he have to come up with ways they can use it with other lumber they're buying? He'll do it. Does he have to find new accounts who are looking for just this product? He'll find them. Orphaned projects and thankless tasks are a great opportunity for exhibiting your creativity and demonstrating your perseverance. When they land on your desk, consciously find ways to do both as you tackle them.

## A DOLLAR ABOVE

Of course, Bill Peck doesn't just meet his quota for skunk wood—he sells it at a dollar above the price set in his schedules. When a salesman conveys genuine excitement for a product—perhaps simply because he or she has found the hook that will get someone else interested in it—it's infectious. When you're convincing people about your skills or your wares, honesty and electricity still go a long way.

Tap into these when you can, and turn them to your advantage as you prove how good you really are. Go-getters, by essence, compete against themselves, not against benchmarks or colleagues.

## THE BLUE VASE

What is the blue vase? For you, it's that impossible project that lands in your lap, that seems to have nothing to do with your job or your priorities, that comes from nowhere and pushes you to the limits of your energy, your resourcefulness, your problem-solving, and your morale. It steals time. It puts a wrench in your other projects. It distracts you from your successes and reminds you of your failures. But, most important, it is the opportunity of a lifetime. Unlike the assignment to sell skunk wood at odd lengths, the blue vase is—from the start—a test for something bigger than you even realize: for a promotion or for a chance to be a manager. How can you tell when a project is a blue vase, and should you treat it any differently than selling skunk wood? Sometimes, as was the case for Bill Peck, you'll find yourself answering to your boss's boss or working on a project that stretches you well beyond your normal scope of work—a clear sign of a quest for a blue vase. Skunk wood tends to get passed from person to person in an office, or to get sold by everyone and not by a hand-picked employee who is being tested for the future. When you sense that an assignment could be a blue vase, you'll want to muster all your skills and excitement and *courage* for the job. You can prove yourself selling skunk wood, and end up selling a lot of it for the rest of your career. But when you get a chance to prove yourself by capturing the blue vase, you get a chance to lead a company.

## THE RIGHT QUESTIONS

Bill Peck has learned after years in the army and on the selling lines that asking the right questions can gain you valuable time under pressure. Don't let yourself get caught up in a charge to action without getting the relevant facts that can spell the difference between success and failure, especially when the stakes are as high as your career. What precisely is your charge? What do you need to deliver in order for your work to be considered a success? What can you glean about the obstacles ahead before you fall into them? What pieces of information are unknown or missing? Imagine if Bill Peck hadn't asked for a description of the blue vase— could he have found it when it wasn't at the address Cappy had given him?

## EXHAUSTING POSSIBILITIES

Persistence doesn't mean anything if you don't exhaust 100 percent of the possibilities on your way to meeting a challenge. Before you assume that you've contacted every person on your list, rethink your list. Have you narrowed yourself without realizing it? Have you missed a vital piece of information—perhaps not as simple as a "missing *h*," but possibly as potent—that could get you an audience with the person who could help you realize your problem-solving plan? Before you assume that every "no" is final, try again with a new approach that's tailored to get around the obstacles in other people's paths. What's important to the person you're trying to convince? How can you move them to help you? What could you offer to him or her that would disarm their reservations or make it easy for them to say "yes"? Use your frustration to refocus yourself: What has given you success in the past? What values or skills have worked for you before? How can they be applied in this situation? Brainstorm new approaches to keep your options and your energy high.

## Killing or Filling Time

It's remarkable that anyone, faced with the exhaustion that comes with tackling impossible challenge after impossible challenge, could see anything but a well-deserved nap in a moment of downtime. Yet, Bill Peck sees a chance to finish up a project that could, if he wanted, have been delayed. But he didn't want to delay it. He knew that if, by some chance, he didn't succeed in getting the blue vase to Cappy, it wouldn't be an excuse to hand to Skinner when his report wasn't filed on Monday morning. And he knew that, even if he delayed it with good reason, Skinner would remember the delay and not the report. Unfortunately, when we don't fulfill our promises exactly as we make them, it's the failures and not the successes that stick in most people's minds. Find ways to prove yourself—and recharge yourself—without losing sight of the day-to-day responsibilities that your supervisors and customers trust you to fulfill.

## TRUSTING UP AND DOWN

One of the greatest moments of tension comes when Bill Peck realizes that he cannot assume that he has won Skinner's trust despite all of his great work at Ricks Logging & Lumbering Company. Trusting up and trusting down provide the foundation of any great management team, but we all have boundaries on the trust and confidence we can gain from our supervisors, colleagues, employees, and customers. At some point, you'll be faced with a situation in which no amount of history or belief will get you through: you'll be on your own. To do so, *you* will have to trust that those around you aren't acting vindictively, jealously, or judgmentally; usually, in fact, they're just doing their jobs. If you prove that you deserved that trust, you'll most likely have it the next time you ask for it.

## DELIVERING THE GOODS

At the end of a series of obstacles, you still need to find the means to communicate your success. But, is it always worth chartering the plane and stopping the train? When you're carrying a blue vase, it is.

Bill Peck didn't know it, but the window for delivering on his test was constrained by the failures of those who had been tested before him, rather than by Cappy's travel and party schedule. You won't know how you're being judged until after you ace the test, too. But you can be sure that the decisions you make along the way will be considered successes as long as you know what the most important aspect of your quest is.

## THE DEGREE OF THE BLUE VASE

You've gotten the blue vase and delivered it, too—now what's next? Another set of tests and another set of opportunities to prove yourself. At each job you may only get the test of the blue vase once—if you're lucky. But with each new promotion and with each new company, you may find yourself looking for the blue vase once again. One of Bill Peck's great shortcomings as he battles against his obstacles is forgetting that he isn't the first person who has been tested at Ricks Logging & Lumbering. Once he's succeeded, he shouldn't make the mistake again. Peasley and Skinner, themselves holders of the "Degree of the Blue Vase," can and will be his greatest allies after Cappy Ricks himself.

## IT SHALL BE DONE

If there's one moral to take away from *The Go-Getter*, it's Bill Peck's slogan, "It shall be done." Nothing can better summarize the determination, the endurance, the loyalty, the passion, and the personal responsibility of a go-getter. Kindle it in yourself and all shall be done.

# ABOUT THE AUTHORS

A native of San Francisco, PETER B. KYNE was a prolific screenwriter and the author of the 1920 bestseller *Kindred of the Dust*. His stories of Cappy Ricks and the Ricks Logging & Lumbering Company were serialized in the *Saturday Evening Post* and William Randolph Hearst's *Cosmopolitan* magazine. He died in 1957.

Historian ALAN AXELROD is the author of the business bestsellers *Patton on Leadership* and *Elizabeth I, CEO*. He lives in Atlanta, Georgia, with his wife and son.